Becoming the Better Employee: From Resume Submission to Business Basics

Becoming the Better Employee: From Resume Submission to Business Basics

J Ford

2011

Table of Contents

About This Book

There are thousands of books out there written to teach people how to be managers, but few have information designed to help the employee. New management research results and techniques come out every day and are taught in nearly every educational establishment across the globe and they are becoming more technical, and more detail oriented. Organizations are competing more and more in a global market, and must adjust how they are managed, marketed, and organized if they are to succeed. The success of these organizations lies greatly with the professionalism and support of employees.

Many of the new management books out there seem to teach what the "old school" managers would call common sense, and in today's fast paced world we must take the time to re-visit our old school sense of pride, ethics, and position ownership. In my personal observations I have seen a trend that makes me believe that employees are not as focused on their jobs as they once were. Today's employees seem to be less concerned with what they can do for the organization and more concerned about what they can get out of it, and how well they can play the system without getting fired.

Our culture, in its ever increasing pace, seems to be guided more towards self-gratification and less by concern for the "other guy". We see this everyday just driving home from work when we are cut off in traffic, or when the guy next to you can be seen cursing at you just because you are driving only five miles per hour over the speed limit instead of fifteen like he is. As consumers we seem to demand only the highest levels of customer service and courtesy, and care little about providing the same to others.

This book is designed to help the employee to understand how to succeed at being a "worker bee", how to help increase the productivity and pride in his or her work, and to understand why some organizational leaders make some of the decisions that they make.

I provide examples that show how even the smallest expenses can quickly add up, basics of ethical behavior, dealing with conflict, and why things like tracking work related activities and accepting concessions are good business practices and not personal attacks on the employee.

My goal is to provide an introduction on how to be the "Better Employee" with hopes of benefiting all organizations through improving an employee's understanding of what is expected of them, and to help them understand how every employee has a part in helping the organization be successful.

If we are going to compete in the global market and help our economy at home we need to do more than "Buy American". We need to support our organizations from the bottom up, and becoming a better employee is where this must start.

About the Author

Mr. Ford has spent his working career practicing what he presents in this book, and has held positions in sales, manufacturing, and the service industry as both an employee and as a manger. He holds a Bachelor Degree in Organizational Management, and has spent much of his personal time studying business and exploring business concepts.

He was invited to and accepted the voluntary position of Mentor with his current (at time of publishing) education provider where he mentors fellow students in areas of business and provides his knowledge to assist people who are entering or working in careers related to his background and experience.

Mr. Ford offers customized article writing and *PowerPoint* course creation for business, as well as many other writing services related to business, and is also involved with professional level recruiting, and providing human resource services to both businesses and individuals.

A former colleague writes;
"James is a very knowledgeable, meticulous and professional"
"His first priorities with his work have always been safety and quality. James takes the time to mentor other people that are new to work at hand with patience and skill rarely seen in today's industry. He is also quick to learn new tasks/skills, quickly becom-

ing the high standard of excellence any industry would be proud to have. For anyone searching for manager, technician or trainer there is none better in aerospace. He wholeheartedly has my unconditional recommendation for any position he seeks."

Release of Responsibility

In today's world we must include a clause in nearly every advertisement, or a statement with every product or service that releases the originator of liability should the product or information be misused or misunderstood. It is the same for authors who are trying to provide helpful information...

The information in this document is intended to be a guide to help employees and organizations but is not intended to replace current policies or requirements. Each individual is responsible for researching his or her organization's requirements. The author will not be held responsible for the actions of any individual who has purchased or read the information provided in these pages. Information in this book is the opinion of the author and may not necessarily be that of the majority.

Chapter 1
The Application Package

Searching for work can be very frustrating indeed, especially when there are often hundreds of applicants for a single position. The odds seem to be stacked against you unless you "know somebody who knows somebody".

For those who are fortunate enough to already have a job while seeking a new position, there are some advantages. Someone who is already working can afford to be a little more selective about what position they might take, and what organization they might choose to work for, but not everyone has this luxury. For many, locating a source of income is a necessary priority. Families need to eat, and children need to have new shoes for school.

Submitting resume after resume without ever getting a response is not only frustrating, it can make a person feel less worthy or can contribute to low self-esteem. As difficult as it may seem, you must not lose hope, and remember that it isn't anything personal.

Getting past that first resume screening line can be very difficult when you are one of more than one hundred people competing for a single job. To complicate matters, more and more jobs are becoming specialized which means the screening team will be looking for specific experience within your resume. Human resource teams for large organizations seldom understand the position they are screening for because they are never out there on the factory floor, and many organizations are choosing to outsource this part of their human resource group.

Still, your only good shot at getting noticed will be through your resume and the documents that you submit to support it. This is the first step in getting in the door and your submission package must represent you and leave a good impression.

No matter what you decide to submit or not submit with your submission package, take the time to understand the position that you are applying for and emphasize your experience and talents associated with that position. Using a single generalized resume for every job submission will significantly decrease your odds of getting that first interview.

You will find all kinds of "professional" advice on formatting a resume and whether or not you should have a cover letter or include details of your work history with your resume. Some selecting managers will like to see a great deal of detail on a resume, even if it means writing a four page document, while other managers will prefer a brief single page overview. Unfortunately, unless you know the hiring manager personally, you will probably not know his or her preferences.

Please allow me to offer a few suggestions...

1) No matter what type of submission package you are putting together, please make sure it is free of spelling and grammatical errors. You will be selected in part on your ability to be professional in your work, and your submission package provides the first impression of this ability. Check it once, check it twice, and then have someone else check it again!

2) Take the time to target everything in your submission package to the specific position or career that you are seeking. If you are interested in, and qualified for more than one position or career, then by all means submit more than one candidate package. If you cannot take the time and consideration to focus on the potential position or career, how can the selecting manager expect you to be able to focus on the job that you may be selected for?

3) The submission package should consist of a Cover Letter, Resume, and a Summary of Work.

4) DO NOT LIE ON ANY OF YOUR PROVID-ED MATERIALS! If you are not honest on your submission package, how can you expect to be trusted in your work? Background checks will often be completed, and your inability to perform in the position will be evident. Submitting false information in your submission package can result in the loss of your job, and an automatic rejec-

tion in consideration for future positions. It can also be very costly to the organization that hired you, and to the recruiter that placed you in front of the organization for consideration. DO NOT consider a dishonest submission package as an option to get you in the door. This has the potential for closing many doors to you in the future.

The Cover Letter...

Do not overlook the importance of a good cover letter. Use your cover letter to introduce yourself and to sell yourself to the selecting manager. In a few short paragraphs, explain who you are and what you can do for the organization you are applying too. Don't forget to suggest that they contact you for further details. Yes, they know to do this, but it helps to plant the idea just like a product commercial that says "buy now". Keep your cover letter to a single page, and target the position you are seeking.

The Resume...

Keep your resume to no more than two pages. Additional and detailed information can be provided on your cover letter and your Summary of Work. The information you provide on your resume will of course vary, depending on your education, experience level, and the position you are applying for, but you do need to include the following...

- Objective
- Education
- Summary of Qualifications
- Brief Work History
- Awards & Achievements

The order in which you place the information is not significant and selecting manager's preferences will vary. With today's emphasis on training, certifications and education, I personally like to see this directly following the objective, and then the summary of qualifications to follow next.

It may be difficult for some of you to resist the urge to place every detail of your past accomplishments onto your resume, but resist you must! Select the accomplishments that you feel are the most significant, and that apply to the position you are seeking, and save the others for you summary of work. Your selecting manager does not need to see on your resume that you know how to use an open end wrench if you already told him you are certified in building car engines, and he or she will understand that you know how to turn on a computer if your degree is in computer technologies.

Summary of Work...
The summary of work can provide an area to show your significant growth and accomplishments in your previous positions. Use this area to show how you advanced in your previous positions and to summarize your significant accomplishments. If you do not have a significant work history you can also use this area to emphasize your educational accomplishments. Have you excelled in any groups or clubs at your school? Have you been awarded any special recognition by your instructors or did you manage to maintain a 4.0 GPA?

The Summary of Work should be kept on a separate file from your resume because not all selecting managers will initially be interested in this information. By sending it as a separate file it will be available if the selecting manager chooses to review it.

In the past, I have been directly advised by a hiring manager to include a Summary of Work showing the progression of my career when at the time I did not have a Summary of Work available. With that advice I added the information to my resume and was then advised to cut my resume down to the basics by a different hiring manager. As you can see, the information a selecting manager wants to see is going to be based on the individual preferences of that manager.

A sample of a paragraph from a Summary of Work could be;

Western Ice

07/1982—08/1987—Production Manager

Responsibilities & Growth...When I started with this company they handled both ice and poultry, and I was the lucky one who cut the poultry before it was packaged for the customer. I learned to become a route truck driver when one of our drivers became injured, and with no experience I ran the truck route. I quickly became a fill-in driver for every truck route and knew every customer by name. I also learned every aspect of manufacturing and in a short time became the production manager. The company moved away from poultry to focus on ice and I helped to grow the customer base and improve efficiency in the manufacturing area considerably.

The Interview...

I have been on both sides of the interview desk. I have been the selecting manager, and I have been the candidate being selected. Neither side of the desk is without at least some level of anxiety.

Prior to attending an interview, be sure to do a little research on the organization that you are interviewing with, and if available, it is a good idea to know who will be conducting the interview and the position this person holds within the organization.

Doing a little research will help you to understand a little more about what the company does, its history, and what it may be planning for in the future. It may be helpful in your decision making to know if the organization is world-wide or local, and knowing if the organization is financially sound can help determine your future. It is also helpful during the interview if you can show some understanding of what the organization's goals are, and how you might fit in with helping to attain those goals.

Knowing who you are interviewing with can be helpful too. If you are interviewing with the selecting manager you may need to prepare yourself for more technical questions, while a preliminary interview with human resources may mean a list of questions pertaining to your personality, level of education, and you're your compensation needs.

Bring a few copies of your resume and background information with you to the interview if you are interviewing in person. Having a small handout packet shows that you took the time to prepare, and are ready to provide the information that is needed. If you have any letters of reference or recommendation, include them with this handout.

The person doing the interviewing and candidate selection must be careful to find someone who will be a good match for the position, and more than education and experience must be weighed. The selecting manager must consider...

- Does this person have the required education?
- Does this person have the required experience?
- Will this person be satisfied with this position?
- Will this person require financial assistance for relocation?
- Will this person fit in with the culture of our organization?
- Does this person have a history of jumping jobs?
- What level of communication skills does this person have?
- Is this person self-motivated?
- Can this person work independently?
- Will this person require continuous guidance to keep them working?

As the one being interviewed, you too need to be asking questions and learning about the person and organization that you may be working for. Remember, this is not a one-sided decision making process. You need to be learning, and asking yourself if this organization is one that you truly believe you could have a future with, and this includes deciding if you would be a good match for the available position. You need to consider things like...

- Will my personality clash with that of the department manager?
- Will I be able to meet the expected level of output for this job?
- Does this position offer sufficient growth opportunities?
- Will I feel challenged or bored in this position?
- Will the work shift present any problems that cannot be overcome?
- Is the compensation/benefits package acceptable?
- Is the job location acceptable?

Ask for a business card from the interviewer, and be sure to thank him or her for the time they took out of their busy schedule to meet with you, and follow up with a short email the next day, showing you appreciate being considered for the position, and that you are available to answer any further questions that might be needed.

Chapter 2
Ethics

Ethics may be one of the most difficult areas of our lives to understand. Perhaps we will never understand or at least fully define a strict set of ethical rules to be followed either in business or in our personal lives. This is why most organizations will have ethical guidelines, but not ethical standards in a strict sense.

Naturally, anything that is in violation of the law is unethical right? Some of you may answer this question with an absolute and uncompromising yes, while others are thinking something more on the line of how "that just kind of depends".

Our personal code of ethics comes from many influences throughout our lives, and since we did not all come from the same families, the same parts of the world, or the same economic levels, we will probably not all have the same ethical values.

Someone I once referred to as a friend is a very good example of how our personal ethics can be different even within ourselves. The person I speak of had just finished telling me how throughout his working career he made a habit of taking things from his place of employment because he felt they owed him more than just a paycheck.

He spoke of taking fishing lures from one employer and all kinds of hardware for his car projects from another. At the time we spoke he was laid off from his position and had been trying to contact someone from his place of employment to bring him home some additional hardware that he needed for another project he had been working on.

Our conversation turned to how I was trying out one of those "on-line" movie rental places and how they would send me a movie copy and when we finished watching it we would return it for another copy. He became practically irate with me and told me that my doing this made me no different that the people who had only months before broken into my home and stolen practically everything of monetary value. I tried to explain that I was paying for a legal service, while the people who took my things paid me nothing, but he could not get past calling me a criminal for participating in a fully legal service, while justifying his own admitted routine thefts from his employer.

In business we can run into equally confusing situations. Our managers and leaders preach to us about quality first, and the importance of ethics. They tell us how important it is to never hide a mistake or cover up any issues with a product because we must provide our customer with only the best possible product or service.

In my previous organization, Imagine my astonishment when one of my team members pointed out a damaged part on an assembly and the team leader responsible for that assembly told my team member that he would make sure the damaged area would be hidden so that it would not be a problem!

Even worse was when I took it to the next step. Without telling anyone of the previous results, I pointed out the same damaged part to a manager who in turn notified the manager of the previous team leader. This manager sent a couple of employees to do a better job of hiding the damaged area behind a panel. Fortunately, when I reported this action to my own leadership, the issue was corrected and the damaged part was replaced.

When we make an ethics based decision we draw upon much more than the current information we have in hand. We also draw from our culture, our personal experiences, our training, and even our current attitude which in itself could be influenced by recent ethical decisions made by our peers, or our leadership.

In a perfect world, the same decision would be made by the same people in the same situation every single time, but this is not a perfect world. In the real world, even you will have varied decisions, sometimes based solely on how your day is going at the time. It is easy to argue that you will always hold yourself to the highest of ethical standards, even when the other guy does not, but is this really the case?

If you wake up in the morning and everything feels perfect, you are wide awake, your breakfast smells and tastes extra good today and you know this is going to be a great day, will your decisions reflect that? If you climb out of bed late because the alarm didn't go off, the bathroom light burns out when you flip the switch, you stub your toe while replacing the light bulb, there is no hot water for the shower and there is no time for breakfast, can you say it will not affect some of the decisions you make that day?

The point is that the decisions we make every day are influenced by many inputs, and before we get too frustrated over the decisions that are made we need to take a moment to realize that we may never know all of the reasons a particular decision was reached.

This holds truer as an employee. Just like us, our managers have certain rules to work by and goals they are required to meet. Your manager may have different inputs to weigh into a decision than you do which will influence the decision that he or she will make.

Before you jump to the conclusion that your manager or co-worker is unethical, try asking yourself a few questions...

- Is the condition or decision going to compromise safety?
- Does it have the potential to cost the company money?
- Was the situation or condition clearly communicated to the manager?

If it is not something serious, would it jeopardize schedule and cost to correct, or would it be more cost effective to document the problem as a variance on this unit and then make sure the communication channels are in place to prevent reoccurrence?

Many of us will consider ourselves ethical just because we do our best to make sure we are providing a quality product or service, but there are other ethical decisions we make every single day that affect our employers and reflect on our level of ethics.

When you are hired by an employer you are most often given a set of rules that you are expected to adhere to, and in return for your compliance and your productivity you are given an agreed upon wage, and in most cases, some type of benefits package.

If these rules state that you are to report for work at 8:00 a.m., take a 15 minute break at 10:30, a one hour lunch at noon, another 15 minute break at 3:00 and then go home at 5:00 p.m. then this is what you are expected to do. How many of you will show up before 8:00 a.m. but not really start working until 8:05? Then maybe you take an extra minute or two along with each 15 minute break, and at lunch you may be back in your work station or at your desk on time, but it takes you an extra five minutes to get back to work?

In the above situation we have now cheated the company out of 15 minutes of work. Not a big deal right? This company can surely afford to cover for an extra 15 minutes! Those 15 minutes becomes an hour and 15 minutes over a 5 day work week, and over a year with 45 weeks of work we have now taken more than 56 hours from the company. How many employees are working with you? 1000 employees doing the same will cost your organization 56,000 hours and at an average rate of only $12.00/hr this becomes $672,000.00!

Is it ok to take a few things home once in a while? Many of you will draw the line here. That is stealing! Isn't using company time for personal business doing the same thing? How many will not realize that stealing time is often more costly to the organization than stealing paper clips or ink pens, but let's take a look at that. We will use some easy numbers to figure with, assuming that we have the same 1,000 employee organization and each person takes home a single $1.00 item each week on average, with 45 working weeks out of the year. That will be $1,000 / week, or $45,000 / year!

My point is that being ethical not only helps to maintain good standards, it saves the organization money, and saves jobs. Many organizations are moving a portion of their work to foreign countries not because they want to, but because they are being forced to. They must cut costs in order to compete in the world market, and much of this cost cutting starts with you and your personal level of ethics.

In many of the professional ethics courses you learn about the importance of not taking bribes or kickbacks, and how dumping toxic waste illegally can harm the organization as much as the environment, but we are going to stay focused on something more controllable at the worker level.

Have you ever stopped to consider the ethics involved with how you treat your fellow employees? Did you know that unethical treatment of your co-workers, even when not crossing the boundaries of the law can be detrimental to productivity? Why should you care? Go back to those figures on how time can cost you your job!

When at work, act professionally and always afford your co-workers professional courtesy. It doesn't matter that you think Joe is a scumbag, or Jill is the office gossip, they are co-workers who have an important role to fulfill or they would not be there. Keep in mind that what you see on the surface may not be all there is to this person, and the work assigned to them may not be the same as what is assigned to you, or other co-workers.

It is always good to remember that just because you do not see a co-worker turning that wrench or punching keys on the keyboard doesn't mean that he or she is not being as productive as you are. Maybe you don't see the difference in the assigned tasks, or maybe this person struggles in an area that you don't but may excel in areas where you do not. The point is there is no need to make accusations, or think that you are expected to do more than the next guy. You need to stay focused on you! Perform your tasks to the best of your abilities at all times and you will be successful.

If you do see a co-worker struggling, check with your supervision and ask if you can help them. Maybe your experience has taught you a few tricks to make the task a little easier to deal with, or maybe there is a simplified way to transfer that data from one screen to another that your co-worker is unaware of.

To be judgmental and accusatory of fellow employees creates unrest and tension in your work area, and is not conducive to a productive or harmonious work environment. Have you ever worked in an area where you can feel the tension in the air just because of a certain individual's presence? Try not to become that person!

Are there times that you should worry about what your co-worker is doing? Of course there is. If you suspect that your co-worker or someone you know within the organization is acting outside of the law or outside of company policy, and can get someone hurt or cost the organization money or its reputation, then do not hesitate to report your suspicions to your supervisor.

Be careful when you are discussing business, company products or services and organizational goals outside of the workplace. It is easy to get caught up in frustration or excitement and feel the need to share it with your friends and family, and today's availability of social networks, e-mails and text messaging makes sharing easy. Just remember that some information from work may be proprietary, and that no matter what, once you have pushed the send or share button, what you have said cannot be taken back. Don't get yourself fired over a comment sent in a moment of frustration!

Chapter 3
15 Things to Remember

1)   *The organization does not exist, nor was it created just for you to collect a paycheck.*

People do not invest in a business without the hopes of getting something back from that investment. Even a non-profit organization has a goal to help a cause. If the business cannot reach its goals, chances are your job will go away. Helping your organization is helping yourself.

2)   *Most organizations are built to make a profit and if that goes away, then so does your job.*

If you cannot be productive enough for the organization to yield an acceptable return on the stakeholder's investment, chances are the organization will either close, or move to an area where it can be cost effective.

3)   *No matter your position, your pay, or your experience level, you can and will eventually be replaced.*

Never allow yourself to believe that you are not expendable. You learned everything you know through training and experience, and so can the next person.

4) *Always be your own worst critic and put a little pride back into the heart of your organization.*
    Just good enough to get by isn't good enough if you want to beat out the competition and help your organization to excel.

5) *The organization owes you nothing more than what your agreed upon contract provides.*
    The organization hired you to provide a service to them and you were given a wage and benefits package that you agreed upon prior to coming to work. Taking home parts, tools, or office supplies is nothing less than stealing.

6) *Good or bad, the actions and/or words of one, really can make a difference.*
    Have you noticed how in a group, if one person will take the first step towards the table, others will follow? Be the one to take that first step towards making your organization both profitable, and a better place to work.

7) *Protect your organization and your organization's resources as if they were your own.*
    Saving on the utility bill, being efficient and maintaining compliance with applicable rules and regulations protects your organization and the profit it generates. This in turn, helps to protect your job.

8) *An organization that is not capable or willing to change is a dying organization. Be willing to learn and adapt with your organization.*

Technology, culture, environment, customer demands, and just about everything else in the world is constantly in the process of changing. If you want your organization to succeed, you must be willing to change and adapt to the changes that influence your organization.

9) *"It is not my job" must not be in your vocabulary.*
See number 8.

10) *No matter the consequences, accept responsibility for your actions.*
Nobody likes to take the blame for someone else's mistakes. If you cannot be responsible for your own, you do not belong in the organization.

11) *If you cannot respect the person, at least respect the position.*
You do not have to like the person you are working with or the person you are working for, but you still have a job to do and that person has a job to do too. Put your petty personal differences aside and be a professional.

12) *Tolerance should always be a two way street.*
A good organization embraces diversity. To the organization this diversity means opportunity for new ideas, and combining different ways of thinking into the best possible service or product in the most efficient manner. Learn to respect differences, and expect others to do the same.

13) *Your perspective will most likely never be the only perspective in a group environment.*
Be willing to listen to the ideas of others. Seeing things from a different view can lead to new ideas and accomplishments.

14) *Management is not always right, but then neither are you.*
Your managers are people, just like you. The decisions they make are made based on the information they have available to them, and you do the same. Not all decisions are easy to make, and not all can be made using clear and complete information.

15) *As a member of an organization you are a part of a team. A strong team is made up of individuals who are willing to step in and support, and provide guidance to fellow team members.*
Understand that just like in sports, your leadership will need to draw upon the strengths of some, and overcome the weaknesses in others. Be willing to compensate when needed, and to step aside when asked. The organization is not all about you, and you do not need to carry the organization solely upon your shoulders. Rely on your team.

Chapter 4
Communicate Effectively

No matter where you go or what you do, effective communication is linked to success and poor communication can be linked to failure. It does not matter what industry you are in, you cannot provide a good service or build a good product if it is not effectively communicated what that service or product is to be and how it is to be performed or built. Effective communication is important at every level of an organization, and equally important when communicating outside of your organization.

As a consumer I am sure you can easily recognize the importance of good communication skills. If you communicate that you want a burger and fries and you are given chicken and coleslaw it can be very frustrating. Did you communicate your order effectively? Were you provided feedback so you could verify that the order was understood? We see examples of poor communication nearly every day. From drivers failing to signal a turn, to the written instructions in the assembly manual that came with our latest purchase of an overseas product, poor communication practices have an impact on our daily activities. How often do you find yourself speaking to a foreign customer service office when you are trying to figure out a product or billing issue with a company you thought was here in America and cannot get a resolution simply because of the communications barrier?

Some organizations will have established communication streams such as written instructions for completing a task, formal training classes, and daily informational meetings led by your supervisor. Most will also have an "open door" policy that encourages employee feedback.

Chances are that the person or persons writing the task information for your organization is not going to be as familiar with the actual task as the person performing the task. If there is something wrong or at least questionable about the task instructions, make sure you address this with your supervisor. This portion of the communication process is feedback, and feedback is a necessary part of the effective communications process. If the task instructions are not corrected, or made to be clearer, there is risk of completing the task incorrectly. Depending on the task, this could result in an unsatisfied customer, hours or re-work, or even the death of a co-worker or customer in the most extreme circumstances. Imagine what could happen if your task is to install the high pressure lines that are used to send pressure to lower the landing gear on a large passenger aircraft but the task did not tell you to tighten the connections for these lines! Maybe you tightened them anyway because it just made sense to do so, or maybe you did not because you assumed that an upcoming task may cover this. It is best to not assume, find the answer.

In a formal training class we rely heavily on the instructor to communicate the intended message. You may think that in this situation the communication process is only one way, but is it? Do you have a test at the end of your course to show how well you understood the message? Will you be demonstrating what you have learned in a "hands on" environment? Did anyone ask for clarification to any part of the training, or did the instructor encourage participation in what was being communicated? These are all forms of feedback which provides the instructor with a return message that answers whether or not you understood the intended message.

Communicating with management at any level must also be effective. A manager must make the decisions that will affect the operations of the business, and these decisions are based on gathered information. If the information provided to your manager is honest, complete, and effectively communicated, your manager has a better understanding of the situation and his or her decisions can be more effective.

If a manager must base his or her decision on incorrect or incomplete information, it will most certainly affect the outcome of the decision being made. A good manager will appreciate your honesty far more than you telling him or her only what they want to hear.

In my most recent position it was common to see team leaders tell their managers that everything was on schedule when in fact they were working around part shortages.

In some instances the team lead of one area would tell the manager that the assembly had been moved to the next station when in fact it had not been. This would build a strain between department leaders because the pressure would be on the receiving area to complete an assembly that they did not yet have.

Effective communications between co-workers is critical on tasks that require more than one person to complete. Do not assume that your co-worker already knows what you are thinking, especially if the task involves any work or issues that are not routine. Communication between co-workers can increase efficiency and can prevent people from getting hurt.

If you are a part of a two person sales or marketing team tasked with contacting all of the local businesses that are on a provided list and you do not first communicate with each other on how to approach the task, you may both end up contacting the same businesses. This not only wastes time and effort, but it could also upset the organizations that you are contacting and will reflect on your organization's level of professionalism.

On the more extreme side of things, let us say that you work with explosives for a living and as a two person team you are tasked with the destruction of several outdated explosives. Part of this process might include securing the items in a pit and vacating the area for one person, and setting up the triggering device for the second person. If the two do not communicate well, there is a very real risk of detonation while one person is still securing the explosives.

The basic communications process is not difficult, but if you are a student in college you may find yourself with entire volumes to study over a sixteen week course just on this one subject alone. In most cases, if you follow the basics you will do well.

- Decide on what it is you want to communicate.
- Select a median for the communication (face to face / formal meeting / e-mail / etc.)
- Identify your target audience and prepare your communication using words and methods that are understood.
- Try to eliminate distractions that will disrupt or interfere with the communications process.
- Deliver your communication and encourage feedback.
- Assess feedback to make sure your communication was understood, and re-communicate if it was not.

Something you need to keep in mind about written communication is that it provides a permanent record of what has been said. Be careful when using email, a memo, or formal letter. Rather than being accusatory, you can use words like, *it appears that,* or put what you are trying to say in the form of a question and do your research. Always be ready to back up your statement with evidence if needed.

A communication from an employee to an upper level position that questions a decision, or tries to correct a misstatement should only be sent after you have evidence to support your statement, and must be sent with consideration of the position the person holds. I will never question a decision unless I know that it could negatively impact the organization, and that I have evidence to support my opinion. I will never tell a superior outright that they are wrong. It is best to offer your opinion, and remember that although the decision may affect your department, you are not the one ultimately responsible.

Chapter 5
Deploying Common Sense Cost *Cutting*

There are a number of programs out there that are being implemented throughout organizations across the globe. Some are used as tools for organizational improvement in certain areas, and some are more encompassing and cover the entire organization in all areas of improvement. Many of you have heard of most of these programs and have been frustrated by the millions, if not billions of dollars that are spent on them in the name of saving money. *Six Sigma, Total Quality Management, Kaizen, Lean Manufacturing, and Just in Time,* are some of the terms you have probably heard.

All of these employ rules and tools that are designed to improve efficiency and cut costs for your organization, which is required if your organization is to successfully compete in today's market. If you would like to know more about these programs in detail, I encourage you to go to the library or book store and pick something up on each program.

It is my opinion that much of what these programs do is to teach and encourage what should be common business sense that many organizations have gotten away from.

They teach us to generate less waste, decrease our inventory, align our tasks more effectively, listen to the employees, and to always be looking for ways to improve our processes. With all of these programs, a little common sense goes a long way, and be careful to not take them too far.

Six Sigma for example will give you tools designed to study a process and measure the benefits of changing a process, but do you need to spend the time and money to put together a team and perform a detailed study to show that if you turn out the lights when you leave the office you can save on electricity?

There are certain benefits from what *six sigma* offers, including a good understanding of how changing processes can improve your organization and it is a great tool when examining complicated cross functional team projects. If you have the opportunity to be involved with a *six sigma* team I recommend that you participate fully, but use caution. Remember that it is about reducing cost for the organization, and if your process change simply moves the cost from one department to another, it saves the organization nothing. All affected departments should be represented when a *six sigma* project encompasses multiple areas of the organization.

Without *six sigma,* you can go a long way with simple common sense techniques like keeping the parts and tools you need to complete a task near the work area, or organizing the steps within a task, and the tasks themselves into a logical and efficient order.

Kaizen is a term that simply means continuous improvement. You should never stop looking for ways to improve the efficiency and safety of your area. Keep in mind that new people to the area can offer new ideas and outside views may offer new insights that you couldn't see. Be open to input from others.

Does it take the implementation of *Lean Manufacturing* to understand that putting your tools away where they belong helps to organize the area, or that keeping your tools near the work area rather than in the next room saves time?

It should not take an expensive program to tell you that having to repeat work due to poor planning, or repairing assemblies due to poor work instructions or worker error is costly to the organization. Taking ownership of one's area can go a long way to help your organization get lean. Treat your area as if it was your own small business and the costs are coming out of your own pocket, and your organization will be better organized and more cost effective.

Every aspect of business should be well organized, from the management structure down to the building layout and tool placement. The business should focus on uniformity to allow for ease of movement from one area to the next with the least amount of disruption. If you see ways to improve your area or your organization as a whole, communicate this to your leadership.

As an employee you can help your organization succeed by staying organized and by becoming knowledgeable and efficient in your assigned tasks. Take ownership of your area and treat it as if it were your own area of business.

Just as any other business, chances are you have suppliers (you get your parts, software, or information somewhere), customers, (internal or external, your completed task does not sit around just for you to admire it), and you have the tools or supplies you need to perform your task.

Communicate with your vendors if you have issues that need to be resolved, and ask for feedback from your customer to see if there is anything you can do to improve your product or service. Keep your tools and supplies well organized and keep your work area clean. Doing so will help you to look and feel like a professional. It will also help a great deal when those pesky auditors come around.

Knowing what you are working with can go a long ways when it comes to improving your efficiency. Do not stop at learning how to put the parts together, learn what they do. If you learn how something works and what its function is it is easier to understand why it is important for some things to be a certain way. It will also be easier for you to recognize possible defects, and make relevant suggestions for improvements.

Chapter 6
Stay Up-to-Date

It is easy to get into a routine and steer away from looking at your drawings, or task instructions after doing the same thing over and over again. Do not allow yourself to get into this rut.

Check your drawings and work instructions regularly for possible changes, and if you see anything out of the ordinary with the parts or documents that you are working with, question the change. The earlier in the process a mistake is identified the less it will cost to fix the problem.

If your position requires certifications or regular training intervals, do not allow yourself to fall behind. Not only could there be changes in regulations or requirements that could affect your performance, internal and external auditors may be periodically reviewing employees to verify that all training and certifications are up to date. Depending on who the external auditors represent, you not being up to date could be costly to the organization.

Knowledge is an incredible thing, keep expanding your knowledge and become the best you can be at what you do, and you can make a positive difference for your organization. Your level of quality can increase considerably when you know what you are working with, and what its function is.

In addition to improving quality you may be questioned by auditors or potential customers about your product or service and an informed response can help show the level of professionalism within the organization that you represent. Knowing what you are doing helps a little with the boss too!

For most of you, there will be trade magazines or journals that are specific to your industry or specialty. You may also find articles and websites on the internet that address your area of expertise. Read up on the latest developments or changes to regulations that affect your organization and the area of your specialty.

You may also be able to find organized groups and organizations that are dedicated to improving areas within your industry. Some of these groups may send out newsletters or offer annual trade shows where people from your industry can get together and learn from one another.

Chapter 7
Accept Change

In order for your organization to succeed it must be continually searching for more efficient processes, new products or services to offer, and new ways to trim expenses. Sometime this will mean changes for you, your department, or even the entire organization.

Contrary to what some workers seem to believe, an organizational change is not designed to single out certain individuals or groups and find ways to make their lives difficult. Organizational change takes place to improve the organization and to better compete with organizations within the industry. Departmental changes and changes in task organization are also designed to help the organization compete, and without the ability to change, the organization will be left behind.

It is interesting that many of us will want to have the most up to date cell phone, music player, or fish finder, but when it comes to change in the work place, there is a tendency to resist.

Much needed change throughout the organization can sometimes be blocked by employees who refuse to accept the changes. The sad thing is that these employees will feel they are victorious when change fails, and then do not understand why they are on unemployment a few years down the road.

For a long-term successful career it is beneficial to be involved with successful organizations, and you can help make your organization successful by being willing to adapt and accept that change is a way of life, and a way of being successful in business.

Chapter 8
Concessions

If you are a member of an organization that does business in the global market, you may eventually find yourself having to deal with what is known as concessions. I am sure you may have heard of what concessions do without maybe hearing the term.

Many of our workers unions will complain that complying with concessions takes jobs away from American workers, but in reality, accepting concessions often adds jobs to the American work force.

When seeking opportunities to build a product and sell it to foreign nations, it is important to understand that many countries have laws that require such sales to include some type of work for their own citizens. Because this is law for that country, if your organization does not consent to concessions, your organization does not get the contract and you and your fellow employees get no additional work at all.

A simple example could be that your organization builds airplanes and you want to sell one hundred of them to country "A". Country "A" says they will buy one hundred airplanes from your company if you will allow country "A" to build the tail section of the airplane. Your organization has the option to refuse and not sell one hundred airplanes to country "A", or to accept, and keep people working for a few more years at your organization. Many of today's worker's unions will protest the decision to allow the concession with hopes of saving jobs, but in actuality, not allowing concessions means losing jobs.

Chapter 9
Employee Conflict

It is inevitable that at some point in your career you will find yourself having to deal with conflict. How you deal with this conflict or potential conflict will say a lot about your level of professionalism.

It takes two or more people to participate in an argument. Know when to walk away. Proving how tough you are by standing your ground or allowing yourself to get caught up in the emotional aspect of the situation is not the way to impress your manager.

You may have to work with people who have a negative attitude, thrive on conflict, or feel as if they must make their co-workers look bad in order to make themselves look good. How you deal with these co-workers and the situations that arise around them will say a lot about your level of professionalism. You must be able to recognize who these potentially difficult co-workers are and understand that people such as these may not be attacking you personally; it is just the way they deal with things.

I will never forget my grouchy old grandfather who did nothing but complain. I am not sure that I can say that I ever heard a kind word come out of his mouth, but still, I knew his intentions were good. I am sure you know or have known people like this yourself. People like this in the work place are not much different.

You may feel that your co-worker spends more time finding a reason to not do something than they do getting something done, or you may believe that your co-worker can only communicate by making you feel inferior. People like this may never provide a positive comment, and may make you feel uncomfortable. I have worked with individuals who can generate tension in a room with their very presence. It is up to you to understand that no matter how bad this person may seem it is most likely that your co-worker does not have ill intentions.

Your level of professionalism stands out when you have the ability to overlook the negativity of your co-worker and maintain a conflict free work environment.

If you do find yourself in a position where you believe you are being pushed into a future conflict or feel as if you are working in a hostile environment, speak to your manager about it. There may not be any immediate solutions available, but your manager's awareness of the situation is important. Remember the chapter on effective communication?

If it seems that your manager is unable to help, seek help through your human resource team if needed. There is little worse than hating the idea of going to work every day just because of the stress that is placed on you by a co-worker.

Chapter 10
Leaders vs Managers

You do not need to be a manager or supervisor to be a good leader. If you know what you are doing and do it well, chances are you will become a leader. The leadership I refer to is not an assigned position for the organization; it is leadership that is earned through respect. The textbooks call this "Expert" leadership.

Expert leadership refers to your ability to influence co-workers and supervisors alike because you know what you are doing. If you maintain a high level of professionalism, communicate effectively, and keep up to date on your industry, you will be respected for it.

OK, so now you are asking yourself if you get paid any extra for this and why should you put out the extra effort if you don't. Chances are you will not get paid extra for this, but you do get paid, and you get paid because you were hired to do a job. It is your responsibility to provide a quality service to your employer. In effect, you are in business and you were selected to provide work in exchange for an agreed upon amount of compensation, including benefits. If you want to be successful as an employee just like you would want to be in business, then make the extra effort.

In today's world you will likely find yourself in an organization that does not always promote from within. Your manager may be experienced when it comes to managing people, but may have little experience in your professional field or with the organization. To help your department succeed you may be called upon to help your management understand the what, how and why of what your department does. Be ready to help those above you just as you would help those around you or below you.

New co-workers will need to be trained and you have the ability to influence their future with the company by taking the time to instill in them the professional attitude that you have developed for yourself. This not only affects his or her quality of work, but will also affect the organization as a whole.

You may not consider your small position within the company very important, but no matter what your position, if you take it on as a professional should, you have the ability to send out ripples just like the pebble in the water. Your expert leadership can influence managers and co-workers alike, and they will in turn influence those who are around them. The attitude that blames everything on management doesn't cut it. Every single worker or manager within the organization has the ability to make a difference and influence the success or failure of the organization and it starts with you.

Chapter 11
Health and Safety

An organization is made up of people, and people care. You will hear time and again that the company does not care about its people, especially when you are with a large organization, but keep in mind that the "company" would not exist without people. The organization was once thought up and created by people, and it maintains its existence through people, and people do care. Maintaining a safe work environment should always be one of your primary concerns. Healthy employees are happy employees, and happy employees are good for business, so why wouldn't the company care?

Nobody knows your work area better than you. Take a look around your area and evaluate the tasks you perform every day to see if there is a way to make it just a little bit safer.

Are you trimming trees with a chain saw and a ladder? Think about using a strap on the saw to sling it over your shoulder so you can have both hands free for climbing, and then secure the ladder and if possible, yourself to the tree. It would not be good to have a branch swing down and knock the ladder out from under you!

Are you going to work on your car this weekend? Take a few extra minutes to block up your car before you crawl under it. Never use only a jack to support your vehicle. Also remember that if your car was driven recently, it may be a little hot under there so be careful where you touch, and even areas that may not be too hot to touch may still contain hot fluids.

Does your factory job require drilling, cutting, or the use of numerous tools of any kind? Take the time you need to organize your area for safety. Tools on the floor become trip hazards. Even a small wrench when stepped on can cause a serious accident. Keeping your area clean not only helps to keep your area safe, it also says a lot about your level of professionalism.

- Rags and cleaning solvents in the area of heat or electricity can become fire hazards.
- Extension cords and air hoses can become trip hazards.
- Steps without railings can become a fall hazard.
- Tables with wheels that are not locked can roll away when someone leans on them.
- Dust and metal shavings can cause permanent blindness.

In most manufacturing or maintenance areas and in many service industries you will be required to wear safety glasses and / or hearing protection. Wear them! Do not take chances with your eye sight or hearing. Loss of either can affect your quality of life and that of your family as well.

Are you spending your work hours at a desk? Make sure you get up once in a while to move around. Sitting for long periods can cause problems with blood flow. Getting up and changing your focus for a few minutes can also help refresh your mind and improve your thought processes. Be mindful of your sitting position, and if keep sharp objects put away when not in use. Remember, even a paper cut can be painful enough to impede your work progress.

You will hear talk or maybe eventually participate in what is called a risk assessment. This is often used when evaluating a potential new project or project modification. It involves a little brainstorming on what could potentially go wrong, and the likelihood of it happening. Survey your area and perform a quick risk assessment of your own. You may be surprised at what you find when you take the time to think about it.

When you think safety, think beyond yourself and your co-workers. Think about your families and friends too. How will an injury to you or a co-worker affect the people you or they care about? Isn't putting forth a little extra effort and taking a little extra time to be safe and ensure the safety of a co-worker worth preventing the potential risk of a costly life changing event?

Chapter 12
Bridging the Gap

In some of your larger organizations you may feel as if there is a definite gap between hourly and salary workers. You may get the impression that hourly workers are thought of as being less important to the organization or are thought of as a lower class of people. In some organizations this may be true for some people, but never forget that not one person is more important than the next, and it may be up to you to help bridge the gap between hourly and salary.

Every single person in the organization has a job to do and every job must be completed with the highest level of professionalism. From cleaning toilets and sweeping floors to making the controlling decisions for the organization, all positions play a part in the success of the business.

Be a professional in what you do, avoid acting as if you need a babysitter instead of a manager and you can bridge the attitude gap between hourly and salary employees.

You are all on the same team and helping the organization to meet the same objectives. You may have a different role to play on the team, but you are working for the same end results nonetheless.

Chapter 13
Getting it Right the First Time

An important part of taking your position seriously and being a professional is reflected in your ability to perform your tasks correctly. If you are unsure of what to do or what your task is, ask someone. Do not act as if you know what you are doing if you do not. Remember the chapter on effective communication and the importance of professionalism?

Organizations can spend millions of dollars because an employee somewhere early in an assembly skipped a process, and this can affect multiple organizations, as well as the end user of the product.

Something as simple as using an incorrect rivet in a small part that is destined to other manufacturers can result in very serious consequences.

Imagine that you work for a small business that supplies a part similar to a turnbuckle, except that only one end of the turnbuckle adjusts and the other end has a connector that is held firmly in place by a couple of rivets with an extremely high sheer strength. A new employee in your business did not know the difference between a standard rivet and the one that was called out for this special application, and built a few hundred of these parts incorrectly.

Now imagine that these parts were sent out to your customers who use your parts in applications where safety of the end customer relies on your part to hold together securely.

Imagine again that the end customer has already purchased some these assemblies before it is determined that the incorrect rivets were used in the assembly that your small business provided.

Now your customer may have to recall the products they have sold and rework the products that have not yet been sold, and these costs will most likely go back to the supplier of the faulty part.

As you can see, something as simple as installing the wrong rivet can be costly to not only your organization, but also to your customers and to your customer's customers.

The same can be said if your small business is responsible for writing contracts, training documents, or task planning and someone gets the wording wrong.

Imagine a work instruction that says "drill three ¾" holes at ¼' intervals" when it should read "drill three ¼" holes at ¾" intervals".

Getting it right the first time can sometime mean the success or failure of your business.

Chapter 14
Tracking Your Data

It is possible that your organization will want to track your performance, work hours, training, and even document your mistakes. Do not panic! Many organizations may be required to track your time spent on the task due to a customer contract, and even if this is not the case, it is simply good business.

To increase efficiency an organization must be able to gather data on almost every aspect of the operation. Knowing how much time you spend on a task can help them to understand budgeting. Knowing how many mistakes you are making will help them understand your need for training, new tools, simplified task planning, or the need to place you into a position that better suits you. Knowing what you are trained for and your efficiency level in a task will help the organization when it comes to organizing the work load and in shifting workers to compensate for unexpected events such as part or personnel shortages.

In most cases your performance is not being tracked so that the company can find reasons to fire you! The information ties in with effective communication, planning, and continuous improvements that will increase the efficiency of the organization and help keep you and your co-workers working.

Chapter 15
Discrimination vs Diversity

Diversity in the workplace is a necessity, but for many it can seem frustrating and confusing. For those of you who have been passed over for a promotion in order to maintain or create a diversified employment base it can be tough.

Many may be asking how it is possible to have diversity and equal treatment in the same organization, and although you may never feel it is fair, it is something you must accept.

Who gets the promotion is not always about qualifications or experience and in a world full of discrimination where we are told that we must ignore race, ethnicity, religious preference, and whether or not you are a man or a woman when it comes time to hire or promote, diversity can be very confusing. It has been ingrained into most of us from a young age that discrimination is a bad thing, and to select or refuse friends, club members, employees, or elected officials based on anything other than merit is wrong. Seems simple until you add in the need for diversity, because diversity brings the focus back to those things you have been taught to ignore.

One of our early chapters in life teaches us to see everyone as the same, but when you turn the page to look at the next set of instructions it says we must focus on and embrace people in the workplace based on the same things we were once taught to ignore.

If you have been in the same position for the past ten years, filled your degree requirements, were patiently awaiting the time for your boss to retire so you can step up, you would most likely become upset if when your boss left he or she was replaced by someone new to the company and fresh out of school. Guess what? Now you get to train your new boss because she has no experience on the job!

Have you then been discriminated against? Based on what we learned in the past it could be, but today we say we are promoting diversity and it works.

Perhaps the organization decided it needs to have more women represented at the management level, or maybe it just wanted fresh ideas, and who better to see new possibilities than someone who has not been previously associated with the daily routines of the organization. No matter the reason, this is the way of modern business.

For some of you this is the cause of great heartache, and for others it is cause for hope, but for everyone, it is a fact of life that must be accepted. Perhaps one day we will truly become equal in all aspects and no longer recognize people as anything other than people, but that is not the world of today and maybe it never will be. We hire and promote based on someone's background and a person's culture is part of what makes them who they are. It is a tough subject to say the least and will be for many years to come.

Diversity in the workplace means more than meeting government regulations or proving to the world that your organization is an equal opportunity employer and should not be embraced for these reasons.

Diversity in the workplace means bringing new ideas and new perspectives to the organization that can offer great opportunities for increased productivity, better designs, and improved marketing techniques.

Each of us comes from different backgrounds, different families, and even different parts of the world. We have unique experiences, education levels, and cultures to draw from, and therefore have the ability to offer unique perspectives in many situations.

If you have been a part of an effective product improvement team, your team may have been made up of workers from the production line, leadership, engineering, finance, supply chain, and maybe even marketing. This is because the best way to address possible change or improvement is to have input from different perspectives.

People from different areas will have different perspectives on what can work and what cannot. In this case you have each area that may be affected by the change or improvement represented because each area can provide the ins and outs for that phase of the change, but it is a good example of how diversity works.

Let us say you have a stack of ten square blocks on a table, each block is numbered one through ten on one side, five of them colored white on another side, five of them colored black on one side, and all of them colored a different shade of blue on a third side. A fourth side of five of the blocks has pictures of men on them, and the other five has pictures of women on them, with the remaining sides left blank and the color of wood.

Now you ask five different individuals to organize these blocks, one person at a time. One may place them in numerical order, while another may place them according to the blue shades going from lightest to darkest. A third person may group all of the white together and all of the black together, while yet another may separate the men from the women. The fifth person could choose to group the men and women together as couples. This is because each person has a different perspective on how the blocks should be organized based on their own experiences and backgrounds.

Try putting all five of these same people together in the room with the blocks and have them organize the blocks as a team. The results could be interesting, and it could take a series of long discussions before a final decision is made, but for certain, each person will learn something from the other. This learning process and having the ability to choose from all of these different perspectives is what diversity is all about.

Stagnation in an organization is a bad thing, and if we do not bring in new ideas and new ways to see how we are doing business, or how we could be doing business, stagnation is what we can end up with.

Chapter 16
Outsourcing & Job Migration

Outsourcing is moving work that is normally performed by your organization to another organization, or hiring contract labor to come into your place of operations to complete the work, most often for a lesser cost to the company.

Job migration has become more common today just as outsourcing. To cut expenses, get away from high taxes, labor costs, and increasing regulations, some organizations are moving all or part of their operations to other countries. This is why you may sometimes find it difficult to converse with your organization's payroll or customer service department, or why you might read about how our country is reducing its manufacturing footprint.

There has been much concern about outsourcing and big business in the United States moving the high paying jobs to other countries in an effort to cut costs. Some people blame corporate greed, others blame poor management that prevents U.S. organizations from being able to compete in today's world market. Maybe some of the problem lies in our own inability to perform well enough to give the organization the edge it needs to survive and compete on a global scale.

Workers are becoming more and more frustrated with new rules and programs that they do not understand. As we become a more technical and politically correct workforce, we seem to be creating a gap in knowledge and growing unrest between the management level and worker level within some of our organizations.

Programs designed to improve efficiency and increase the profit margins while at the same time help to lower costs are being implemented in organizations across the world. Today's college students are taught how and why these programs work, but little is passed down to the strong backs that keep the organization driving forward.

Business leaders and managers give orders that drive change within an organization but do not seem to take the time to tell people why the changes are being implemented or to explain the overall plan for the organization's survival. The size and fast pace of many organizations leaves workers feeling as if they are nothing more than a number in a book, and this feeling contributes to a decreasing work performance.

When organizational leaders see work performance and worker's attitudes become increasingly less desirable, and watch profit margins slip and their ability to compete with others within the same industry falls, action must be taken to survive. This can mean outsourcing work to other companies, or even moving jobs like yours to other countries.

Managers tend to blame workers and workers in turn blame managers and corporate officers for the lack of profits and the loss of jobs. This blame slinging only helps to build bigger gaps between the two groups and adds to the underlying problem.

In some cases it may be true that an organization cannot compete because of poor management and there will always be cases of corporate greed that will drive decisions within the organization, but I like to believe these are the exceptions and not the general rule.

Another contributor to this dilemma is the ever increasing government controls that are being placed on U.S. businesses. Regulations keep stacking up against the organizations and they often bring with them high costs of monitoring and/or implementation. Some organizations simply cannot afford these additional costs, and others lash out like a teenager who is struggling for his or her freedom and decides to leave the controlling household.

Worker's Unions can take a little of the blame for forcing companies into outsourcing or sending work outside of the country too. Much like the government pressures an organization from the outside, unions apply pressure from the inside telling the organization how it must do business. Unions drive up labor and compensation costs, while at the same time protect the nonproductive workers which gives the company little or no recourse other than to continue to pay the workers who fail to contribute to the company. This is frustrating for both the organization and the productive workers as well.

While most unions will advertise that they work with and support the success of the company, they will also begin plans to strike against the company long before negotiations have begun. It is human nature for the organization's leadership to respond to threats with a strong defensive stance. Imagine how things might go if the union would begin talks with an open handshake rather than a closed fist.

It may be time for our workforce to step up to the plate and decide to make a difference. You can't change the ever increasing government regulations (unless you get out and vote), but you can ask yourself if you are contributing to your fullest potential. The more productive and efficient a workforce can be, the better the organization can support the workforce. It is a two way street.

Workers can make a difference in the organization and in the national economy. A growing, efficient, and productive organization puts people to work and keeps them working, which in turn increases spending and further economic growth. An organization cannot be productive without a strong and supportive workforce.

Are you ready to make a difference?

Summary

Becoming a better employee is all about becoming a professional at what you do. It doesn't matter where you work or what your job is, taking your responsibilities seriously earns respect.

When you become a better employee, you benefit as much as the organization. Do not allow yourself to fall into the trap that drags you into asking why you should do well for somebody else, because you shouldn't. You should be the best you can at what you do for yourself. You need to be able to feel good about what you are doing. Just getting by is not what work, or life is all about and it gains you very little.

We tend to blame organizational leaders when a business fails, or blame greed when jobs are sent across borders. Maybe it would be a good idea to take a look at ourselves before we blame others. Are we doing all we can as employees to help our organization compete in today's market, or are we simply taking advantage of our employer and collecting a paycheck?

Our society seems to be more and more self-centered. We often focus on what "I" want, or what "I" can get by with. We want to do something or have something just because the other guy has it. We justify not giving our all because the other guy doesn't. After all, why should you work hard if Joe and Jane don't have too right?

It is time to stop worrying about what the other guy is doing and start making a difference. Protect your job, your future, your family, and your self-worth by becoming a better employee. It may not be too late to help keep some of our jobs right here at home!

www.ingramcontent.com/pod-product-compliance
Lightning Source LLC
Chambersburg PA
CBHW022132170526
45157CB00004B/1846